Signs and Abominations

wesleyan poetry

# Signs
# &Abominations

## Bruce Beasley

Wesleyan University Press    published by

university press of new england    hanover and london

Wesleyan University Press

Published by University Press of New England, Hanover, NH 03755

© 2000 by Bruce Beasley

Printed in the United States of America

5 4 3 2 1

Grateful acknowledgment is made to the following journals, which first published some of the poems in this volume: *Boulevard*: Hermetic Diary; *Denver Quarterly*: Advent Unprayer; *DoubleTake*: January 1958; *Fence*: Negatives of O'Connor and Serrano; *Field*: Spiritual Alphabet in Midsummer; *Gettysburg Review*: Errata Mystagogia; *Iowa Review*: Fragments from Judas's Gospel; *Kenyon Review*: The White Children of Macon; *New England Review*: Pomegranate; *Ohio Review*: Hermetic Prayer; *Ontario Review*: Hyperlinks: Incomplete Void; *Ploughshares*: What Did You Come to See; Mutating Villanelle; *Sulfur*: Hermetic Self-Portrait; Sermons on Unbelief; "Errata Mystagogia" is reprinted in *The Pushcart Prize XXIV: Best of the Small Presses* (2000).

for Suzanne and Jin

the overlay

of the sacred

*And behold, Thou wert within, and I abroad, and there I searched for Thee; deformed I, plunging amid those fair forms, which Thou hadst made.* —Augustine

# Contents

# Acknowledgments

Thanks to Tim Liu, Dan Tobin, Bill Wenthe, Robin Hemley, and Rosina Lippi-Green for their friendship and advice. And to the Artist Trust and Western Washington University for grants that were enormously helpful in writing these poems. And to Mary Anne Berg Richardson for her advice on the history of Baconsfield Park.

*Forerunner*

# What Did You Come to See

Jesus began to say unto the multitudes concerning John, What went ye out into
the wilderness to see? A reed shaken with the wind? . . . But what went ye out for
to see? A prophet? Yea, I say unto you, and more than a prophet.
—MATTHEW 11: 7-9

There's always something sepulchral
John the Baptist wants us to see, something
that will ravish us more than he will—

see how he gestures (forerunner)
toward the timeless, sacred scene,
leading, if you follow him, the eye

away from his muscles and camel-hair rags,
hung pelts of his robe, the black wilderness skin—
and the corrected,

redirected gaze
moves over the canvas, to the Virgin
and Corpse with arrow-

ridden, ghastly saints,
ageless, toothed
cleavers stabbed inside their haloes.

The pointing Baptist is always there
only not to be there, to exempt
himself from the scene of redemption,

so he glares straight-on and his finger
begs us not to look at *him*,
which makes me gaze all the harder

at his honeycomb and locusts, his thin
reed cross: What did you come
to see, a reed

shaken in the wind? Icon
of not looking, of returning the gaze
to what lies far beyond the phenomenal—

So, on the highway to San Sepolcro,
roadsigns for miles proclaimed
PREGNANT MADONNA, NEXT EXIT—

Madonna del Parto, in her roadside shrine, restored,
but we still missed the exit, counting
whores, in gold lamé, red

leotards, waving at truckers,
while the signs
pointed, insistent: Piero

della Francesca's Madonna
del Parto, exit, exit . . .
There's always something more awful

the world wants us to see, pointing
away from Christ's gestation
to the dairy truck

screeched into gravel-ruts,
the prostitute's leotard split open at the crotch
as she runs to meet it, and the gaze

redirects itself, refocuses, and the sacred
and its restored
depictions

blur.

~     ~     ~

In Palma Giovane's self-portrait,
he's so mixed in with his scene
of Transfiguration, you can hardly tell

who's the painter, who apostles and saints
with their arms cast out in astonishment
at the Christ blasted off into light:

except that *he* holds the splattered brush,
and so paints his own way in
even as we watch, transfiguring

his life to a scene of the holy:
how should we direct our gaze? to the painter, to Christ,
to the witnesses cowering from the blare

of light? Or look back
from what we can bear to see
to the sign of what we can't,

apostle blinded from the sight. Icon
of unseeable splendor: what
*did* we come to see? A foppish

man in stole and beret, who's stared
for four hundred years, believing
his own brushstrokes could grant him entry to that Kingdom—

Not like the Baptist, all
beast-skin and exposed muscle, no sign
of his martyrdom, no severed head

—emplattered—to show us, who stands
in a wilderness of his own making,
pointing away.

I stared at his finger
crooked toward the business of the cross,
clumped vein over bone in the twisted wrist,

and barely glanced toward Calvary.
Signs, abominations:
it's always the diversion

that attracts me,
what doesn't mean to be seen that I need
to stare down, until it's just dried

pigment on a canvas, ground
lapis lazuli, ultramarine, daubed
strokes in eggwash and squirrel-hair,

something wholly of its own time (truckstop, split
leotard) of which
it keeps telling us: Don't look.

I

# Negatives of O'Connor and Serrano

> ... writers who see by the light of their Christian faith will have, in these times, the sharpest eyes for the grotesque, for the perverse, for the unacceptable.
> —FLANNERY O'CONNOR
>
> God created the body for a reason, and we were meant to exploit it.
> —ANDRES SERRANO
>
> O one, o none, o no one, o you:
> Where did the way lead when it led nowhere?
> —PAUL CELAN

### Negative 1

Andres Serrano would jack off on Jesus

(the congressman said)
if the NEA would pay him to do it—

*What this Serrano fellow did,*
*he filled a bottle with his own urine*
*and stuck a crucifix down there,*

*he is not an artist, he is a jerk*—

—He jerks off
in the air, and photographs
his semen's fretted
transit through space, *Ejaculate*

*in Trajectory,* abjected seed. What leaves
the body. It's substance
he wants, not representation:
blood and cum, milk and Christ, submersible
icons. Black spume all around the Last Supper.
In O'Connor's *bleeding, stinking, mad*

*shadow of Jesus,* cibachrome
Pietà in cow's blood, Jesus seethed in piss—

Strip of negatives, images
stripped down to their substance, stripped of their light.

*Negative 2*

*No truth*, shouts Hazel Motes, *No truth behind all truths is what I preach . . .*

Stains of menstruation
Serrano preaches: used Maxi-pads, cratered landscape of blood.
Plotinus calls the physical world
the font of all defilements and confusions. It's unbodying
we want, *un*knowing, to know a God
*luminous, incomprehensible*

(*Nor is He body, nor has He form or shape*),
the Negative Way to That
Which transcends all affirmation—

Or so says Pseudo-Dionysius.
Jin, in his baby backpack, belly-laughs
at the woman's strap-on dildo
in Serrano's *History of Sex*, already, at six months, knowing
incongruity of breasts and cock—

Via negativa, radical denial:
to strip from what we say of God all that He is not
(*Neither has He power, nor is He power, nor light*)—

what's left's
shriveled, inchoate, known

incongruity of numinous substance and world . . .

**morgue Klux Serrano menstrual piss**

the Internet tells me. Refined
search terms littering the bottom of the screen. Unholy
scat. Unbodying
quest: *Show me where your wooden leg
joins on.* Serrano's
bloodscapes, Hazel Motes'
barbed wire and lime-burnt eyes.

Evil, I read, is nothing

but the tendency of things toward nothingness—
In a world that God made good, iniquity
must be like the zero, a hollow
that in multiplication reduces
everything to itself.

And so this apophasis, this
orbiting of the 0:
We have to approach supernatural grace
negatively, O'Connor says
(*Grace would have to be violent to compete with the evil*

*I can make concrete)*, have to show where it's not, not where it is, tracing
the fretted tracks its long trajectory leaves.

Not where it is. In the Children's Crusade, 10,000 boys
straggled from France toward the Holy Land
(censers, wax candles, oriflammes),
chanting prayers for the Mediterranean

to dry up and let them cross.
At each walled hilltown outside Paris,
they pointed and cried, Is that Jerusalem?
Is that Jerusalem, the profaned

holy land just across the walled-off square,
is *that* Jerusalem, the plastic
Pope smeared with menstrual blood,
tabooed. Unbodying

debodied One, is that
Jerusalem, the chill
sea-wave rushing against those children's feet?
Or the seven

rotted ships that wrecked
halfway to Palestine
on San Pietro, the boy-
pilgrims' bodies washed, eternally

undecomposing, to that shore?

In Serrano's *Auto-Erotic*, the model
licks his own cock,
feeds his cum back to himself,
face lurid in burnt-red light, cheeks
hollowing to suck himself harder—

(*I don't need no hep*, says the Misfit,
*I'm doing alright by myself*)

Self-love, the concupiscent
tongue, cockhead's wet tip:
ache of the torso's contortion,
misfit
of self to self.

Unbodying quest, for substance: *Love Him*,
Meister Eckhart preaches, *as He is: a not-God,
a not-Person, a not-spirit, a not-image*—

The Bible case
crammed with condoms

and a wooden leg. *Deformed
I*, Augustine says, *plunging
amid those fair forms
which Thou hadst made*—

Amid the fair forms, Serrano's
plexiglas Cross full of blood,
O'Connor's hermaphrodite, in its tent,
*God made me*

*thisaway, I don't*
*dispute hit—*

I don't dispute it, the secret,
the secreted
(blood, choler, phlegm, bile),
all things the flesh
can't keep, can't keep

hidden. All
defilements, all confusions:
crucifix lopsided on a mound of chicken hearts,
pickled brains floating in pedestalled vials.
Lashed Christ, tattooed into Parker's back, *haphazard*

*and botched.* Super-
Essential Darkness, God is beyond
any name we can give Him, any image

that would show Him, Dionysius tells us, *beyond*
*all affirmation, all negation . . .*

Monica Lewinsky's
blue semen-stained dress, seized
for DNA tests. Evidentiary claims
on the President's cum.
There are no curtains in the Oval Office.
Newt Gingrich: "Eatin' ain't cheatin'."
*For the purposes of these depositions,*
*an act of sexual congress shall mean*
*any and all genital contact.*
Ed Bradley, on primetime TV:
"When the President placed your hand
on his genitals, was he *aroused?*"
Meanwhile, the plexiglas Popemobile
in Havana. Mass in Che Guevara's square.
Eight-story banner of Christ. Pamphlets
to the people: *The Pope*
*is not a politician, not a tourist, not*
*a magic remedy.* The press's
departure from Cuba to cover the semen spot,
dress hauled off and scrutinized
thread by thread, like the Holy Shroud. Was he aroused.

*Negative 8*

White Christ
purified in a vat of milk.
Hazel Motes: *One Jesus is as bad as another.*

Negatives, darkened texts,
reversed icons, blotched, from which
the representational illusion proceeds, print, and print—

*Of neither the things that are, nor of the things that are not*

From his butcher on 38th, Serrano
hauls back to the studio his gallons of blood

*Neither does He live, nor is He life*

In a dream, even books
are mortal: crusted
tumors on their pages, leeching
fleshwounds on their covers

*Neither can reason attain to Him, nor name Him, nor know Him*

(Serrano's
slammed and jeweled cathedral gates)

Hazel Motes: *Where
has the blood you think
you been redeemed by*


*touched you?*

II

## Hermetic Prayer

"What do you mean, `what
do you mean'?":

black-glazed
hummock of snow, in a parking lot,
shoveled a story
high, still hoards its cold
after weeks of thaw, laving
its walls with twice-frozen
half-melt trickling through sunflash—

but deep, the snow crust
hardens (impacted
detritus of crystal), into
interior
weather, impervious
to weather . . .

Lord, in the penetralia, the hidden
places where thaw
won't go,
verify
all verities (what
do you mean),
slicken, black-
flash, hunker
down, let us

go.

## Advent Unprayer

The roots
of Paradise: "walled
around," not

as I thought
"pairi Deo," around
God.

Around God, the walls, surmountable.
Around God, the litter
of negations (not

effable, not
corruptible, not there).
Always

we're walled-off
by what we can't say,
summing, with each word, the subtractions.

"Pairi
daeza," walled
around. Rooted

there, in the barrier,
splitting
its mortar. Unpray

the way
in: tacit, sub-
linguistic, like

the precatory
insuck of wind-gash
over the gnashed

island beach
(walled-off
by wave and rock-cove,

the dune's spikelets, in windrows,
in salt-harsh air,
parted, as if parsed

by what rushes them).
Long squall brings Advent
in ("ad

venire," to come to, not
"ad ventus," to the wind).
Holy Ghost, come to

us, on this
soaked December wind,
brine-full, lifting

the black sand,
palpable like that.
How to forge

a prayer of it, Lord—
what to make
anymore of words

vestigial
as these: chaplet,
pall, purificator,

quia per sanctam Crucum
tuam redemisti mundum . . .
What to make, Lord,

of the words
corruptible, sub-
tractable, always drawn

away? What to make:
here the water (vinum
et aqua) *change*

*it*: here the wine.

# *Fragments from Judas's Gospel*

### 1.

And Jesus instructed the twelve again, saying
what you understand I will take
from you now like a wound

### 2.

From the figtree, learn its lesson:
it shrivelled, branches to root,
a few hours after he touched it

### 3.

She drew forth the precious alabaster
jar of nard, anointed him
with her hair. The poor (he laughed)
you have always with you.
His feet slathered with the priceless
ointment. All around us,
the fatted lamb, baskets of fish
(Lazarus, corpulent, sprawled at his side)

This is my body, he kept telling us

### 4.

Because they alone understood him,
he would not permit the demons to speak.

For the rest of us, garbled
parables
(The Kingdom of Heaven is like

the rendered
tallow, fat of the lamb;

like the bridegroom
who lies with his bride,

in joy, and then in bleeding)

Meaningless
speech, lest we turn and be saved

  5.

And he marveled
at our unbelief

  6.

Mary said to the angel,
do with me as you must,
only spare my life,
for my sins are grave indeed

  7.

They sat mending their nets
when he called them,
arbitrary. The fishes
slapped at the flat stones, slashed
with their gills.

He who comes with me
will be like this, he said,
and held the stilled fish in his fist.

  8.

The healed lepers
sat by the roadside,
begging, still scraping their scabs.
The healed blind man lay with the flies in his eyes

9.

Barabbas, drunk in the brothel, shouted
Jesus has set me free

10.

He said to Peter, the Kingdom built on your rock
is a desolate kingdom; I will give you its keys

11.

Render unto Caesar
that which is Caesar's,
unto God, that which is God's:
for once, I could obey him, and with a kiss

12.

O you of little faith,
Lazarus is laid again into the grave.
Take your comfort in his going down to Sheol
since your disbelief has made his raising
fail

13.

And Jesus turned to me,
his weeping servant Judas, saying
See you
tell no one these things

# Sermons on Unbelief

Sermons on unbelief ever did attract me—
—EMILY DICKINSON

I.

Good Friday. Blood orange and Billie Holiday.
The cross adored, in the streets: torchlight
on cobblestone, huddles of brown-hooded monks.
Hushed procession of believers. I watched
the bearer of the wooden cross
watch me, through a restaurant's purple curtains:
day of fasting, splayed meat on a plate,
empty beaker of wine. At three,
under the sacred, bell-jarred head
of St. Catherine, I tried, in slurred Italian,
to ask a priest where the services were; he directed me
to the toilet. Service
of redemption: Stations of the Cross
on primetime TV, crucifix of fire on the Coliseum walls.
Then blues, and fruit. Drill-whine and hammer-on-metal
of restoration in San Domenico: we waited
half the afternoon for the services
that never began, and translated
a newspaper story about thirty-nine dead
of applesauce and phenobarbital,
who believed a spaceship from comet Hale-Bopp
would take them to a higher evolution. Hushed
procession of believers. Purple
handkerchiefs over their faces.
Credevano di essere angeli . . .
A priest slapped the paper, told me
this was a place for prayer.

All day we'd been looking for converters
for the blowdryer, the laptop.

Watching souls crawl out of Limbo
at the touch of the harrowing Christ.
Higher evolution. Museum guard,
when we asked her what "castità" meant,
said "non fare niente, non fare il sesso"—
Not doing anything. Not having sex.
The cult's leader had himself castrated.
In the allegory of Chastity, the virtuous
hunch their bodies against Love; Cupid
aims, anyway, from his pit of flames.
Billie Holiday. Non fare il sesso.
The flaming swordtips of Eden,
closed. How Adam and Eve
recoil, even in Limbo, from Christ.
Already harrowed. Telnet
statler.cc.wwu.edu: the longing for e-mail's
transmundane conversion of phonewire and byte.
Lux Mundi. Cybercafe,
500 lire per minute online. Converting
lire to dollars, liters to gallons, lux
mundi to luce del mondo.
The light shone in the darkness and the darkness knew it not.
Mea maxima culpa. *Imagine*
*what an insane cult the Romans*
*must have thought the Christians were,*
*the Son of God flown down from heaven*
*to rescue us from our sins . . .*: Easter feast,
all our talk's about the Heaven's Gate
cult. Castrated faithful heaped in their villa.
Believing themselves to be angels. Non fanno niente.


*II.*


Palm Sunday Mass, Rome, Santa
Maria degli Angeli:
sun-stab through one panel of stained
glass (saint's-face in scarlet) over
the convert frescoed by the altar. Whose arms

grab toward a wingbeat of angels. Sun's
burned circle around the dim
figure, till all I could see
was one hand, blistered toward the angel's
receding flock of wing and gown.
Palms wilted on the pews
of the church converted from Diocletian's
tepidarium baths. Ten people at Mass,
newspapers under their arms. This
is a place of prayer. Convert
eradicated in her ring of fire,
while the little bell jangled in
the Transubstantiation
into flesh.
I'd spent the morning looking for an ATM.
Sportello automatico. Electric
candles in their banks under an altar.
Where the service is. Exposed
buttocks of a guard in Sodoma,
at the base of the cross. Cleft where the painter's real obsession lay.
The body they're hauling down with ropes
and pulleys meant nothing compared to the taut
musculature of the thighs, the near
transparence of the uniform
over the ass. Sodom,
ashheaps, pillar of salt. The Deposition's
a project for engineers, all ballast and angle.
How to get down from the cross. When we learn how to die,
Montaigne said, we'll unlearn how to be slaves.
Hale-Bopp over via Cassia, its tail of endless arrival.
Heaven's Gate on the Internet, click and you'll learn
how to die.

Blood orange. Billie Holiday. Gloomy Sunday.
My heart and I have decided to end it all.
O triumphant holy day. Then another
hallelujah. God, with the Cross in His hands.
Spattered blood at the nailholes. Adored. Bring me a mustard seed,

said the Buddha to a woman whose child had died,
from any house that has never known death, and I'll raise him.
She wandered the city, counting the dead
from each family. Ashheaps, pillar of salt. Kingdom
of heaven like a mustard seed. Dwell in the wounds
of Christ, the *Imitation* advises.
The feat of getting the body down from the cross:
levers, pulleys, ropes, hard
strain in the muscles of the buttocks.
Heaped bodies. Then another hallelujah, and an amen.

   *III.*

Drill-whine of restoration. This
business of bringing down the divine:
Michelangelo's made his self-portrait
in Nicodemus, hauling Christ off the cross. Dwell
in the wounds. Spark
of graphite as he chipped the marred
block of marble. Then smashed Christ's body,
disgusted with the stone that never would yield
the human image. Che bel
marmo hai rovinato. Christ, missing one leg.
In the Gate of Paradise, God and the angels
together yank Eve out of Adam's side. Hard
labor. Already harrowed. Angel wings
hide Adam's genitals, during the Temptation. Not doing anything, not
      having sex.
And it burned, burned, burned,
the ring of fire. Down the divine. Cain bludgeons Abel, Abraham
yanks Isaac by the hair and bares the rough knife to his neck.
What failed human images. Phenobarbital
and applesauce.

Gate of Paradise, replaced
panel by panel with copies.
The door itself is a reproduction now. You can't
trust anything you look at

in Italy, it's all a fake,
my barber said. They're scared
somebody will smash the real statues so they've got them locked up in a vault.
You might as well just look in a book. Resplendent
shadows of Plato's cave. The imitation
advises. Webpage of Heaven's Gate, help thou my unbelief.
Logged on, and on. Shed
our flesh and rise to the mother
ship. Untouchable angel. Mary
hovers over the iron nails through the feet
somewhere in the Uffizi. Touches them, like Thomas.
Annunciation without lilies. She believes. Heaped
bodies, reliquary of miscellaneous saints:
femur, finger, knucklebone. The missing leg of Christ.
Both of Paul's index fingers, in separate jars in one room.
You can't trust anything you look at, it's all a fake.

IV.

Eve, in Masaccio, covers her genitals; Adam, only his eyes.
It's too late not to be naked. Not too late to be blind.
You get fifteen minutes to see the Brancacci Chapel,
with thirty other people (locked up in a vault).
Elbowing for a view of Expulsion.
Trying to remember who paid who the Tribute Money,
why Adam and Eve are in the scene, why Peter's upside down.
Till the guard blinks his light, says it's time, and you go.

All day we'd spent looking for a converter. Old ladies
shoving and kicking their way to the Host
at Easter Mass. This is my flesh. Hale-Bopp,
star-smear over the harrowed field.
I stared a long time to make sure I knew what I saw.
Next to the comet, red Mars. Hail and farewell. Eat this
so that sins may be forgiven. Why not,
why not give them back where they came from, Eve
uncoiling out of Adam's side. Snapped whips of the angels.
The noble Bevesangue, who liked to lick the blood from his sword.

Abraham's jagged knife. Dwell. Blood of the new and everlasting
covenant.

Peter's upside down. The cock
in the castle's barnyard down the street
crows at three in the afternoon. It's time.
Three confident betrayals, and then shame.
Eve in Masaccio, Judas
in any Last Supper. Moneybag tied to his side.
The bread, grained and red in the wine.
Torches, hooded face, splayed lamb,
this is a place of prayer.
St. Thomas, in Orsanmichele,
stumbles toward the hole in Christ's side.
His right foot standing on nothing, overstepping its niche
above my head. That's faith, launching
himself toward proof of the gash, his whole balance resting on air.
Blessed are they who have not
seen, but have believed. Phenobarbital,
shed flesh. He's the merchants'
patron saint. Business of redemption. That never would yield
the human image. That's why
Adam and Eve are in the scene. Sermons
on unbelief ever did attract me
toward and toward (unsteady) the inhuman wound.

III

# Spiritual Alphabet in Midsummer

> The various states of soul in a man must be like the letters in a dictionary, some of which are powerfully and voluminously developed, others having only a few words under them—but the soul must have a complete alphabet.
> —KIERKEGAARD, IN HIS DIARY

*A*

This is the finger of God:

gnat-swarm in fruitbowl, torn
flap of plumskin
riddled with them, blackberry
vinegar, in its open decanter,
thick with swimming gnats—

I walk through the house, laughing
lines from Exodus (I'm teaching
the Bible as Literature
for extra money): *There*
*came gnats*
*on man and beast, all the dust*
*of the earth became gnats,*
*and the magicians said,*

*This is the finger of God . . .*

Hyssop dipped in lamb's blood,
hail and fire in thunder, Raid
Flying Insect Killer's
pillar of cloud over the stove, *I will smite*
*the land of Egypt*—

Jehovah's Witness once at the door,
fat hellflames lapping at the Watchtower cover:
*Lotsa people they think Hell*

*is hot—;*
*but Hell's not hot, it's not, it's not . . .*

Merciful
God, of temperate
Hell, harden
our hearts, this summer, so that signs
and wonders

may be multiplied—
Deadly
nightshade twined around the raspberry canes—
We lick
raspberry juice
from each other's fingers. Black
vinegar swirling down the disposal, compost
bin's sweet reek of fruit,

sprayed gnats dropped on the microwave,
finger of God
on everything, its

smudged, unmistakable print.

*B*

In the year of our Lord one thousand
three hundred and seventy-three,
Julian of Norwich, *living*
*in this mortal flesh*,
felt her spiritual eyes slip open

and she gazed on Christ,
enthroned inside her
*(a delectable and restful sight)*—

serene, implacable, eternally
holding court there
as if her soul *were a kingdom*
*and a fine city*.

Monday, in a dream, mine
was laid bare: hushed
attic room, unfinished, hot,

abandoned window fan's rusted blades
blocking the crawlspace
I kept crawling through,

and frizzled wires
at the end of each passage
hissed and sizzled, sputtering
fire—

*And soon afterwards all was hidden*
*and I saw no more.*

*C*

To learn the spirit's alphabet, its spells

of heat and freezing,
I have to find my way beyond the vowels,

mellifluous containers of desire:
the real work waits in the consonants,
oilslick along the inside of the drum,

smirched smell of what's not usable, not saved.

*The self says, I am,*
says Roethke,
*the heart says, I am less,*
*the spirit says, You are nothing.*

To be nothing, in summer, when sweetpeas
wind strangling around their stick,
when my hollyhocks lift their stalks—
ladder-spoked with pink blooms—as high as the roof

(My place in the world
that is not my place)—

when everything stakes and stakes
its extravagant
claim to being

through rarer and more complicated forms of beauty.

To be nothing, and to want to be that,
diminished and joyed in diminishment,

like the catarrhal
rasp of the poppy's seedpods

hollowed on cracked stems and spewing
thousands of invisible

seeds on the wind that distributes
also their long, deceptive

death-rattle from the dry stalks . . .

# D

*The whole of existence*

*frightens me,*
Kierkegaard wrote in his diary,
*from the smallest*
*fly to the mystery*
*of the Incarnation . . .*

So Serrano's *Piss Christ*: divinity
suspended in human

waste, the nailed body bubbling
down through urine-filtered, mystic

gold-red light,
Incarnation as willed submersion

in what even the flesh rejects—
Kafka's diary: *the joy*

*again of imagining*
*a knife twisted in my heart . . .*

*E*

Twisted knife, dirge-prayer:
watering the starved
garden, the slugs'
beer-traps dried up,

drizzle of slug-trail along the sweet basil's plot.

*F*

O inhabitant of the Earth,

August melancholia, insomnia, dog days
hazed in gray. Tetris
at 3 a.m., in-between
Genesis chapters in *God: A Biography*—
in both, the compulsive
filling-up of the empty. Anhedonic
god, domesticated
in his desert tent, sniffing the wind
for the scent of burnt meat—

His obsession with us, His spirit-life
—rage, wrath, jealousy, vengeance,
displeasure and pride,

never rejoicing—*God does not rejoice . . .*

Who turned to make
no other world,
mad to remain in this one, desert and flood—

I wonder
what He wants from me now,
3 a.m., up thinking
how useless I am, how dull, reading
*I will smelt away your dross.*

—Pleasureless

Lord of Hosts, what remorse, what envy,
stirs in You now,
as in me,

what scrutiny by the dim nightlamp?

*G*

Flute music whose source
I can't find
somewhere inside the mazes

of the purple rose garden—
its trills and slow stops, blown
impositions of order—

while on the sidewalk someone's boombox
hisses news of the bombed-down plane
in Long Island Sound, 230 dead,
scubadivers descending through the lashed

surf to the black box.

*H*

So the tares and the wheat
must grow up together
in their rows, before the harvest,

*lest in gathering the tares*
*you root up the wheat along with them . . .*

Artist's sketch,
in the paper, of the child-rapist:
paroled, then driven
from town to town,
bearded, gaunt-faced, grief-eyed, like
the face of Christ in children's
illustrated Bibles . . .

*I*

*How are the dead raised, with what*
*body do they come?:*

David Gee has willed his skin
to a tattoo artist, all
seventeen square feet of it, in magenta
and pink and brown
serpents and bulls and bats

($33,000 worth of tattoos,
500 hours under the humming knife)

with the one stipulation that it be stripped,
tanned, and permanently displayed

*So that people continue to see me after I'm dead—*

—St. Bartholomew,
in the Last Judgment,
brandishes a knife and trails his flayed skin

on which Michelangelo has painted his own face,
elongated and grotesque in the folds of the pelt.

Self-portrait as shucked flesh,
dragged to the judgment:
Bartholomew glowers, knife aimed at Christ,
or at the Virgin, who recoils
from the damned gnawed by demons, or else
from the raised, damning hand of her Son—

Shall we haul
the flayed skin into paradise
(angels flying the thorn
crown and sponge and pillar of flagellation)

*as long as people continue to see me*
*after I'm dead*

The wrinkled face in the pelt,
the serpent's tongue tattooed behind the ear?

*Flesh and blood cannot inherit the kingdom,*
*nor does the perishable*
*inherit the imperishable . . .*

*J*

Lo, I tell you a mystery:

three thousand embryos, frozen in nitrogen,
unclaimed for five years at in-vitro clinics,

are slated for destruction today
with a drop of alcohol on each.

*We live in samsara*

*and spacing out about nirvana*
*doesn't help anyone*, says

a teenaged Tibetan lama
who's joined a Wyoming street gang
(*if some butthead pulls a gun on His holiness*,
*you can bet some bodyguard's*
*gonna pop a cap*
*in his ass*)

who, between homework and Little League and chores,
sneaks in his spiritual counseling,
*sucking out the bad air*
*and breathing in the pure*

*like an air conditioning repair dude* . . .

Pure air, frozen
nitrogen, three thousand
embryos each the size of a grain of sand.

*A wholly desacralized cosmos,*
I read in Eliade,
*is a recent discovery*
*in the history of the human spirit.*

*K*

By the boathouse's
crumbled pylons,
starfish wallow in low runnels of surf—

when I jab them
with a stick, they clutch it

to their nubbed bodies, trying to take it in . . .

So the numinous
closes around whatever
phenomena happen to stab it,

and clutches,
piece by piece of its star.

*L*

*A universe seething with life*
*billions of years ago—*

NASA on the radio, carbonate
globules in a meteor

from Mars, Earth itself
seeded by supernal life, perhaps.

We hear it as we drive to the Ballard Locks,
where the sockeyes

hurl their battered bodies up the fish-ladder,
its twenty-three steps, artificial falls

that repel and attract their surge.
In the Viewing Room, the salmon

beat their way uptide, through a tank of churned bubbles
like Serrano's four-gallon tub of urine,

haunted by its plastic crucifix:
god who can't leave matter alone, descending

into what craves
transcendence—

and our urge
upward to return to the place

of our spawning—
*universe seething with life*—the sockeyes,

skin ripped, muscles taut with leaping, fight
to spew eggs and milt in a gravel run, where hunks

of flesh will drop off
in the stream where the smolts came from,

once the starved, gill-heaving spawners have driven,
having smelled their way back to its rock.

*M*

Mystery of the Incarnation:

*in my short Pilgrimage,*
wrote Cotton Mather,
*tormenting Pains in my Teeth and Jawes*

*have produced mee many a sad Hour—*

He dedicated that pain
to *search and try* his *Wayes*:

confessing his gluttony, the evil speech
that passed those teeth,
everything razed
by spiritual scrutiny.

And the numbed
gap in my jaw
where a hollowed wisdom-tooth

was plucked today:
painkiller haze, the holy stupor
in front of the TV,

Jeffrey Dahmer on A&E, his barrels of skulls
and rotting genitals
while I thumbed, mind dulled, through Kafka:

*this heap of straw*
*I have been for five months . . .*
*to die would mean nothing more*
*than to surrender a nothing*
*to nothing . . .*

The mystery of the Incarnation:
chemotherapy pumps, angioplasm
balloons,

plastic skull in the oral surgeon's office,
blinking white tooth-lights
like Christmas
around its sunken jaw.

*N*

In my short pilgrimage
through July,

the heat-cracked windshield
of the Mazda,
the cut grocery budget, reruns
of Seinfeld

*filled with the Devotions and Enjoyments*
*of a raised Soul . . .*

*O*

*Why does this generation*
*seek a sign*:
Cross-shaped

blister of sunlight
photographed over a cove
just before three Catholic children

drowned there in riptide: its white
trail of bisecting lights
hung, grained-out and glowing, over the beach.

At the soup kitchen, the volunteers
crowd around a blown-up
print of it, souvenir from the funeral:

*I just don't agree it's the Angel*
*of Death waiting*
*to get them,*

one volunteer grimly shakes her head,
*I don't think it's Death,*
*it's Jesus . . .*

*P*

Walking the dogs,
talking about graces and sins,
docetic heresy and Incarnation,
plastic bags of scooped dogshit
swinging in our hands.

## Q

*Enough is so vast a sweetness,*

Dickinson says,
*I suppose it never occurs—*
*only pathetic Counterfeits—*

Its counterfeits
sate me: stray
Brittany smeared with raspberry
juice, bunches of arugula
and collards, "O
Divine Redeemer," Suzanne,
eating blueberry pie and rereading the Bardo,

it feels so real while Enough
recedes, recedes, hazing.

*R*

RIVERS OF BLOOD IN ATLANTA—

     —headlines
ecstatic in their newspaper boxes:
pipe bomb at the Olympics
while the Heart Attacks played,
a hundred wounded by shrapnel, newsman
collapsed from heart
failure as he ran toward the blast.

In an antique store, beside
porno photos from the '30s
(bare breast under boutonniere)
lies the Sacred Heart of Jesus

in a gilt frame: exposed
from His side, the barbed-
wired and viscid pink heart, a cross
stabbed into it.

*In and through adoration of the physical*
*heart, the threefold*
*love is adored—*

Grease-smell on the hot sidewalk.
We go for margaritas in an empty bar,
her foot in my lap, stroking
my cock as CNN
interrogates the bombsite witnesses,

and the black box
from TWA
is hauled up at last: static
and bomb-blast and static.

Down the block, a hamburger joint
called the Hardened Artery
has another heart on its billboard:

fat, lurid, fed
by rivers of slowed
blood

*S*

*I implore that my Work may be sprinkled*
*with the Blood of the Lord Jesus Christ:*

So Cotton Mather begged God
*with daily Cries*
that the publishers should want his Church History.

—Reading, alongside Mather, my own galleys,
fretting about what the blurbs would say,
what the editors would say,
what the reviews would say,
every night another dream
of the book's
release: *Piss-Christ* on the cover, or my mother's quilt
(in the dream I write it as *guilt*)

or inksmears where the blurbs should be—

*T*

Book of Merits, Book of Faults,
blackened by centuries of candlesmoke:
in the Last Judgment, the fresco's

angels eternally unroll the scrolls,
and the Blessed
quiver to hear their names.

Versions of the holy—
*my agent*
*has three manuscripts of mine, she really thinks I'm hot,*

*you know*
*it's a prestigious award I've just won . . .*

My back
jacket, filled in with its praise

*sprinkled with the Blood*
*of the Lord Jesus Christ*

    —Starfish
wallow in their crack of rock, wrap
their five arms

around whatever seems to them like food.

*U*

Envy: two slugs on a mound
of fresh dogshit,
chewing their way back to the ground.

*V*

If you checked Box 32A, you MUST file Form 2981;
statutory employees, see
page 35, section c

Halfway through Schedule A, 1040
extension till today, and the mail
brings another mortgage increase
and the annual *No*
*appropriated funds for salary raises—*
and I'm hunched again over the crabbed
figures on our budget
        ($960 extra mortgage payments
        minus $750 Bible as Lit
        income)
barely
listening to the bootleg
tape of Flannery O'Connor
in Chicago, 1960: *to track the Holy Ghost*
*through a tangle of human suffering,*
*aspiration, and idiocy . . .*

Deducting infertility,
tithes, cystomeatotomy, psycho-
tropic drugs—

You MUST attach
extension

*Shut up, Bobby Lee, it's*
*no real pleasure in life . . .*

*W*

*For admiring myself,*

*I loathe myself,*
Michael Wigglesworth wrote in his diary.
The unspeakable

conversation of judgment:
In the Sistine Chapel, St. Peter
cocks the round barrel of his enormous
key to the kingdom
and aims it straight at Christ

(*I don't think it's Death it's Jesus*)
who floats
in His yellow bubble,
hand raised in a gesture
of benediction, or damnation, I'm never

sure which. *Munday I found pride*
*monstrously prevailing;*
*Tuesday so much secret*
*joying in myself, plague-sores*
*running day and night . . .*

—All August,
staring at Michelangelo's judging
angels, eyes rolled up in their heads,
I loathe

myself for my self-loathing.
These accounts I can't keep
keeping: sins
deducted from graces, rejections
subtracted from publications

*So that people continue to see me*
*after I'm dead—*

Book of Faults
with a fissure down its middle, as though
the wall itself couldn't bear
the weight of its blame.

                          Lord,
raise Your hand to me now, uncurl it slowly

(*It's not Death it's Jesus*)

release me from judgment till the end of my days . . .

## X

In my Father's house, so many closed-up rooms.
Such slitted attic windows where I find

myself, gazing downward at the garden,
its stunted boles and chewed leaves,

sunflash on the washed and dented Mazda.
In dust-shaft light, dim

buzzings deep in the rafters, over rusted
nails, a cracked jar. Kingdom and fine city.

Lord, rouse yourself for me now, in this sealed
heat, mildewed air, where the soul

hoards its gatherings through the smudged
dust of half a summer, forgotten

souvenirs, windows
gold with another year's pollen.

Sizzle of shorted
wires, spark-flash

like firefly in the far loft: even
here, Lord, in this stagnant attic,

you're nested, driven, swarming
under damp shingles

to a chambered and nectared hive.

*Y*

Liquidation Used Cars'
garbled billboard: *No Credit Check You
Qualify    No Cure for Birth
& Death Except
Enjoy Whats Inbetween*—

         Used
cars: oilslick
under our old
Mazda, the buyer's child
squealing *Mommy Mommy it's
leaking it's leaking*
the truck
in a traffic jam with *Eli
Eli lama sabachthani*
scrawled in its window's crusted mud—

Liquidation: Monarch
butterfly lit
on a decaying possum at creekside. TWA
pilot Kevorkian hauled up
from the sea, the plane's
wreckage on the news again, reassembled
piece by blasted piece. Jack
Kevorkian, Doctor of Death,
wheeling his thirty-fifth victim in,

chronically exhausted, three hundred pounds,
painkiller-addicted, beaten
by her husband for wanting to die.

*Whats inbetween*: wild
blueberry jam's sweet
foam and scum on the stove,
Suzanne, mashing

the berries, her head
thrown back to sing *Libiamo,*
*la fuggevol ora*
*s'inebri a voluttá* ...

Z

How secret
the overlay
of the sacred—tracks
of the Holy Ghost

by the dredged
harbor, the gnarled
and peeled madronas.
Everywhere I look, even

in Andres Serrano's
photographs of the morgue: the lush
scarlets and clumped blacks
of the burn victims' skins,

their hands
blotched with fingerprint ink,
the pictures laid end to end, fingers
almost touching, like God

and Adam in Michelangelo's Creation,
the divine spark reimagined
as flesh-charring. So
*kenosis*: God's

emptying himself of divinity
to take on this marrable
body. Piece
by blasted piece,

the profaned
days are hauled up again,
barnacled and briny,
glinting as they sink

back. Twenty-first
Sunday in Ordinary Time:
I bless myself, and move on,
holy water dripping from my fingers.


*Summer 1996*

IV

VI

## January 1958

So memory would have to begin:
brilliant-edged vase
in the window, its
cold, floating
carnations. A world
stripped
and simplified
to a frayed blanket, rhythm
of radiator-hiss. Scintillant
afternoons, composed
of original
endings: my mother's
hard cough vanishing
down the hall, the gradual
blackening of the window's
pecan tree. Porcelain
skin of an antique doll
beside my crib, its dazed
eyes disappearing
into shadows. Scrape
of my twin brother's
crib bars against mine. Needle
scratching and scratching
the record's last
groove. What doesn't lie
there, in those first,
frostlit twilights, our breath
itself gone white, dividing
from us and rising, the first
time my father strolled
us, in Thomaston,
that 1958 cold
stuck burning, still, in my lungs?

## The White Children of Macon

...for the sole, perpetual, and unending use ...
of the white women, white girls, white boys, and
white children of Macon, to be by them forever
enjoyed as a park and pleasure ground.
—BEQUEST OF BACONSFIELD PARK TO CITY OF
MACON, GEORGIA, BY SENATOR AUGUSTUS
OCTAVIUS BACON, 1914

### 1

In Baconsfield Park, the bear
and the peacock stared
from their tiny cages by the cultivated
bamboo jungle, where we'd play Vietnam,
hurling pecan bombs on the lilypond.
Tadpoles, all bloated eyes,
slipped down through the algae slime.

### 2

Every morning, the choreographed children
of Alexander III
assembled for Macon, as cars
slowed along the park
to watch us skip in concentric circles
around the flagpole, hands
tight behind our backs, singing
*God shed His grace on Thee—*

  *—*seventh-grade
recess monitors
beside me the whole way,
*You're not skipping, you're hopping, keep*
*your hands straight, don't speak*
*unless you're spoken to ...*

We were always circling
something, monitored, heel
to toe: the maypole
rose there each spring,
ribboned, garlanded, its pink
and green streamers waving
under Nottingham Drive's
trellises of trailing arbutus.
Long row of old magnolias, one child
permitted in the limbs of each tree.

3

Gnats, chiggerbugs, river-stink,
mudflats of the Ocmulgee River
where Gray Highway divided Shirley Hills from the black side of town:

my grandfather wanted me to know
why Baconsfield Pool
lay stagnant in heat one summer, chained shut: *Honey,*

*the coloreds don't want to stay*
*in their own neighborhoods anymore,*
*and it's not safe to swim where they go, it's not*

*sanitary* . . . I used to stare
through the fence slats, the pool's
chlorine steam

still rising, trying to burn it clean again.

4

Over the long urinals, the Watchers
gazed on every boy in the class, heads
over our shoulders as we lined up
at the stained marble. Whoever didn't "go"
they sent to Miss Claxton, waiting

yardstick in hand at the lavatory door.

On the blackboard, charts
of who hadn't pissed.

5

The classroom tiered
by how good we were: chosen
Watchers on the front row
by Miss Claxton's desk. In their Izod shirts.
I ranked
toward the far back,
near Masonic Home orphans, the one Jew.

*You could be a Watcher someday, too,*
she'd tease me,
*if only you'd act more*
*like the other boys . . .*

She'd move me a desk backward
every time the Watchers caught me,
and on Fridays, when the lunch money
came due.

And Idas, the black janitor, sat
on his metal pail in the restroom,
in a strobe of broken
fluorescence, where he'd watch
the Watchers.

6

The classes
of Macon: *Tell everybody,* Mama said,
*your father's an attorney,*
*you live in Shirley Hills,*
*you buy your clothes at Davison's . . .*

76

At night, I'd hear them fight, Daddy
hoarse: *don't let us lose the house,*
*just forge your father's signature on the loan . . .*

7

Squeak of the oiled woodfloor, flash
of Miss Claxton's glasses.
I drew my stick-figure family—
Miss Claxton guffawed, *Bruce's*
*mother and father*
*don't wear any clothes, they're nudists . . .*

She'd walk the rows
when I wet my pants,
sniffing, from desk to desk,
till she found me out:
*Is it Bruce again? Who thinks it's Bruce again,*
*class?*

8

*Sole, perpetual, unending:*

When I was twelve, a headline
on the *New York Times*'s front page
read SEGREGATED PARK
MUST REVERT TO HEIRS—
SUPREME COURT RULES. I wouldn't
have seen it: Bacon's
white mansion across the street
was only a place to filch
crabapples, and Supreme
Court just another name
Walter Cronkite would intone,
like Attica, Lake
of Tranquility, Kent State,
while my father

stirred his fifth whiskey, Mama
sizzled the chicken, and outside
the window I
kept up my basketball's
numbing, mantric thump.

9

*I am influenced by no unkindness of feeling*
*for the colored people,* Bacon wrote,
*but by esteem and regard, sincere*
*personal affection . . .*

On Frat Field, in the park, I used to watch
all Saturday the Beta pledges,
hazed in blackface,
Stratford Academy's chosen

class, rivermud and eggyolks dripping from their faces.

10

A phone call
from a neighbor: *We saw a colored man*
*heading your way down the street.*
*We've already checked and he's nobody's*
*yardboy. Don't worry—*
*the police will be right here.*

That was normal
to me, unseeable—
as when Miss Claxton
asked me what Dick was doing
in the picture
of Jane and Spot on the sofa—

*Nothing*, I whimpered, and she
sent me to the cloakroom
till I could see.
I stared for two hours at that picture,
the other children pointing at me
as they gathered their coats
(*Why are you so stupid? Why
do you wet your pants?*)

before I saw, outside
a window, *over*
the sofa, Dick
under a hot sun, mowing the lawn.

    *11*

It's easy to watch now, when I close my eyes,

Alexander III's red bricks
and blackboards
in mounds of wood-shards and splintered windows,
as the steamshovels scraped, and the wrecking ball

crushed,
and McDonald's clownmouthed drive-thru
rose where the maypole had been, dreadlocked
teenagers handing over the fries.

Bacon's heirs had sold the park,
honoring—for a million dollars—
his deathbed wish: that the races
*stay forever separate.*

And Mayor Thompson bought a twenty-ton tank
from the Army, machine-gunned police
riding the streets, warning
through loudspeakers SUSPECTED
ROBBERS WILL BE SHOT ON SIGHT.

Till the pavement cracked under the tank's
weight, and they filled it with flowers
and rolled it
into the city museum.

12

The picture fills in: Miss Claxton,
in the boys' toilet, scrubbing our mouths
when we'd drunk from the yardman's spigot,
then adorning us

for May Festival: roses
and nosegays, lavender
strands of wisteria, timpani
and tambourine (the King
bestowing a pink sceptre
on his Queen), and we clung

each to a streamer, a locus
in the dance, plaiting
and unbraiding the pole, pink
after green after pink
(Miss Claxton's unforgiving eye
on the colors of the braid)
as white

Macon crowded to watch its children
twirl through the steps, hold
to the beat, then skip
in rehearsed circles, hands
safe behind our backs, back

into our class—

## 13

Through the pecan-shaded windows
of Miss Claxton's first grade,
I keep staring now,

down the first row, and the last,
past the Watchers, raising their hands,
dented yardstick hung on its nail.

Behind me, in the park, cicadas
lift their shrill, jittering hum
like a warning, and the flag

thwacks its stars against the pole,
black loambanks crumbling
undissolved into the river.

The class's
window is half-smudged,
pollen-gold. I rub it clean,

and see myself
on the back row, hunched
forward, staring. Ghostly

chalkmarks scratched
all over the blackboard,
white coils and slashes I had no idea how to read.

## Pomegranate

My father, drunk, plucked
its half-ripe heft
from the bush
and cracked it in half in his hands—
its torn
hemispheres raw
and flushed
like something not meant
to be seen. He handed
it to me, his breath
hot with whiskey, his palms
slick from the burst sacs
of juice. The seeds, squeezed
on my tongue, stung
and stained my lips, the rough
rind white and glistening
with exposed, pinkish-wet
caves of pulp and seed—

I was twelve, my body
for the first time
figuring
out what it wanted.
I turned away,

but the sprinkler
shivered
in slow strokes at the Cherokee roses;
their smushed white petals sopped
up a reddish muck

of clay, and sank
under the gangly
figtree, studded
with already

bruised blotches of fruit.

## The Unburied

Aspergillum
of rattled poplar in the rain,

the shrill,
insistent agitations of its crows:

We slip from squall
into sleep, the scraped

excavation of my dream,
and we wander together among

the unburied, the simulacra's
substitutions for lack and desire:

under the blown-down magnolia
my father planted, sacks of muddy jewels;

inside my childhood house,          .
my mother refills her quarts of vodka

with the briny, iv-tube drip of her tears.
And you hold me there, where a protean

grieving twenty years old
transubstantiates itself again and again,

now body, now blood, now torn
crust of bread, dipped in wine (the dug

jewels disintegrate in my hand,
my dead father still lifts the hammer

to my dead mother's mouth)
—And you lead me out

when you wake me, wind
through the deadbolted windows

hissing a sound like *amen, amen,*
while the lashed

tips of forsythia
chop at the bedroom's roof, the skylight's

warped panes scraping
each other in harbor-wind . . . And this

emptied lachrymatory, this
vial of long-hoarded tears

poured out:
in my dream you hold the vial

(it's become my body) and turn
its topaz and emeralds,

its released
tears slick and shining in your palm.

I keep dreaming the word
*lubricious*, its slippery

language-body, its swell
on the tongue,

the slip of my fingertips
over your ribs and slow heart, over

your breast and inward curve of your thigh.
Your breath, in sleep, in time

with mine
till you half-wake me

and stroke my hair,
Suzanne, as you leave

your own dream
of drowning, stand

on shore with your lungs
full of water, so much

care
having always been taken

from us. Aspergillum
of rattling poplar

stricken in dawn-light,
drenched squeal of seagull

in salt-wind and downpour—then swaddle
of comforter, of hands, the kept

time of our undreaming bodies.

## Hermetic Diary

### 1.

       . . . As if lyric
should overtake story, world
shrunken back to a hungering

cry,
its votive-candle words
sputtering their O and their O . . .

Relit, today, at dawn. Invisible
vestibule, where you wait.

Unapproachable
child, when
will you come to us, and on

what plane?

### 2.

Rose moss over rain-garish
brick. As if sequence
should reassert itself
(dim sum, dinner at Lumiere, stared-
down and unringing
phone),
so that things might proceed

into time. So that time
might be no more.

*3.*

Substitutive,

unbegotten:
by Christ's wounds, the five
stigmata,

knot-roses, inward–
gone.

Assisi earthquake: cracked
Cimabue. St. Peter, in crumbled
plaster, unhealable,
healing
the possessed.

The possessive. Who wait. Streaks
of cirrostratus, pulp mill
odor of sopped wood through the window.

Supplicative
barred crib.

Call,
response. I call
you, child, not-yet

known:
blister–
rose the dusk sky

keeps twisting

*(October, 1997: waiting for arrival of adopted son)*

# Hyperlinks: Incomplete Void

> (Calvin's catechism; chronic prostatitis
> Internet newsgroup; *Ecstacy: Shamanism in
> Korea; What to Expect in Baby's First
> Year; Daily Devotional Guide*)

Minister: What thing is that whereby
our regeneration
is wrought in us, child?
A *blood in the semen* webpage
has been created. Opening
of the clogged ducts releases
accumulated infected materials,
bombarded by antibiotics:
Augmentin, Bactrim, Ciprofloxacin. Snake-tracks
in the ricemound
show the soul is not ready for release.
After six weeks the package from Italy arrived,
emptied at Customs and repacked with Biblical tracts:
Daily Devotional Guides. The Messenger from Hell
should be steered toward the table of impure foods:
fatty meats, glutinous rice, broken beans. Front porch
sags in its moss, collapses, woodrot and carpenter ants.
The whole foundation's now suspect. RAGE,
said the telephone pole, GARAGE SALE
stapled around its circumference. Burnt
pesticide smell where the porch was, S-shaped
trail of dead carpenter ants. No tracks
whatsoever in the ricemound
means the soul is befuddled, wandering
without purpose through the underworld.
Daily Devotion: I would blow
the dandelion fuzz toward my son, saying
Go fill the air with Jesus.
Overcome by joy, my boy would run away.
Minister: Was it then needful that he

should take on him our very flesh? Child:
Even so it was. Dad-to-be, have you come
to terms yet with your baby's
finally coming to term?
Kim Jin-Woo, Happy Jewel, born June 17 in Seoul. Signature
on the enclosed forms indicates
final acceptance of adoption decree, pending
naturalization. Then lyeth it not
in our power
to provoke the Father to love us,
or do we thereby only stir him
to yet more wrath? A sensation
of incomplete voiding
may be experienced during acute
outbreaks. Loose-wired car radio, at a pothole,
breaks out from its silence, oracular: Is your dining room furniture
leaving you hungry for more?
Even so it is. Sterilizer,
pacifier, tubseat, basinette. Syrup
of Ipecac, for accidental poisoning. Some Dads
discover changing diapers is more fun than Mardi Gras,
more awe-inspiring than the Grand Canyon. Orgasm
occurs through closure
of the artereovenous shunt
from the pelvic splanchnic nerve to the prostatic
plexus. Verily this cometh to passe
by the wondrous and unsearchable
working of the spirit.
For an FDA-approved device
to make the crib feel exactly like a car
going 55 mph, "complete with windsounds as a soothing
        accompaniment,"
call 1-800-COLIC. This needeth
a more evident declaration.
Daily Devotion: when I was a child, my brother
punctured my arm with a stick.
I kept loosening the bandage to display my injury
to anyone who'd look, which only led to infection

and abscess; Dear God, deliver us from dwelling on our wounds.
With accumulation of purulent materials,
the organ or location must be drained. The shaman must hack and slash
three times through the nine chambers:
underworld, heavenly world, earthly world. A complete
extermination program
must be established in all inaccessible
crawlspaces where nesting may occur. After the last gate,
the soul flies free toward the Western paradise.

# Hermetic Self-Portrait

*avoiding likeness and autobiographic*
*gesture*

### 1

Mid-gut
of the imago, the instars'
moults. And the grasshopper
becomes a burden. In the suburbs, cicadas
seethe from the ground
every seventeen years

(forty thousand from the roots
of one tree)
to breed, and die.
And the empty skins
crackle everywhere underfoot,
tiny golden shells
hung on every surface.

Slough of the tough
carapace, dark thorax, red
front-margin of the wings
pumped full of juice.

Shriek. The ribbed
snaredrums of their abdomens—
the grackles are terrified
by their buzz-saw
song, the neighbors deafened by it . . .

Where am I
in this

emergence—

*2*

Ground punctured with exit holes.
Convulsive
split of the husk: bulbous
eyes, and greasy wings—

This coming
out of oneself, for good, this
leaving hundreds of eggs behind—

This leaving
a finished body behind.

Can a man bear a child,
Jeremiah asks,
the resurrection nymph's

disturbance-squawk . . .

*3*

Can a man *bear*

a child. *Mutare*, to change. From which comes
*moult.* Their music-making
is a mating call, hollow
longing sound like *pharaoh, pharaoh*—

On my parents' tombstone, a dying cicada.
Having bred. It crawled up my pantsleg
when I touched it, the pitched

squeal of its brood around us—

No bouquet
laid down. I'm all out of *white* roses,
the florist had said,

I'm all out of *red* roses, too,
I don't have a single carnation left,

to be honest with you,
I'm plumb out of *every* kind of flower,

I don't even know why I'm here . . .

4

Foghorn
as the music
of insomnia, sounding

all night from the whited-
out harbor
a mile away.

Mist in the nursery window,
three balloons tethered
to the new crib.

In the hall outside,
I stroke my mother's hair,
sealed into her still-life's

oilpaint, stray black S
through the pink carnation,
seventeen years

she's been gone . . . Warning
of the foghorn's hollow
four-second moan,

stilled music
of insomnia, means
of finding ground.

5

Brood. To tell you the truth,
I'm plumb
out of incarnation,
crunched shells
of cicadas, empty
chitinous husks, the nymphs
tunneling into the loam, for a dormant
life.

Long wait
while the nursery fills
with hand-me-downs, with gifts—

(Ground littered with fallen bodies, stiffened
wings)

Staring
at the fog-window,
drag of white, half-visible balloons,

drag of scraggled
lines across the page:

I don't even know
why *I'm* here.

6

Mid-gut
of the imago, the instars'
moults. And the grasshopper
a burden.

*Mutilus*: maimed. Mutation.
Mutatis mutandis, *the necessary
changes have been made.*

Your hurt is incurable, sayeth the Lord.
Your pain is incurable,
and your wounds

I will heal—

So let me come
out of myself, a synchronous
burrowing out of the earth:

black S, still
life, crib's
white balloons, stridulous

cry, *long*
*deep tones in fog or darkness,*
pink painted carnation, seventeenth year

in this emergence. I make the sign
of the cross
over the two names on the grave,

over the belly-up cicada—then its wings
flapping wild in my face, my glasses knocked off—
Bear a child, bear a child

underground, mutable
carapace, twigs drilled full of eggs—
imago, white roses,

abandoned exit
holes, the moult
incurable, necessary: plumb

out . . .

## Damaged Self-Portrait

Then God said, `Let us make man in our image, after our likeness'
—GENESIS 1:26

But tell me, who today has been able to record anything that comes across to us
as a fact without causing deep injury to the image?
—FRANCIS BACON

A shadow on the liver

—what the ultrasound
can't see,
clot of unmappable
flesh, dark mass

unimaged . . .

          So the occluded
self, the always-in-eclipse:
how to draw it

back, as the Infinite
shrank itself out of space, coiled down
to an infinitesimal
point, so that a universe, flawed,
not-God,
might have Its place.
The Kabbalists call it *zimzum,*
contraction, God
ridding the Creation of God,
self-

exilic, desacralizing
the cosmos even as He
gave birth to it—

*Hence we remain ignorant of the true shape of the fireball—*

—Hypernova
erupting in gamma-ray bursts
twelve-billion light years away,

for forty seconds more splendid than all
the rest of the universe
combined,
and no one can even tell

what it is,
what kind of "parent object"
could give birth to such a blast.

We can only measure
its afterglow in X-rays,
the satellite Beppo-Sax
tracing the untraceable
(*Ein-Sof*, the Kabbalists call God, No End, in-
finite, about Whom
nothing whatsoever may be said).

What's
known, what can
be said: Its host
galaxy at a redshift
of 3.42, correcting
for the flux calibration zero-point
and the galactic extinction . . .
Its measured

fluence
(the unknowable erupting out of itself)

and mine:
all the hoarded
silences, crystal
snowdrift
of the unsaid

(and the stubble that rises out of it).

If I could trace
such recesses
in me, so
luminous, so obscure,
could I praise You again,
hosannah, as
a scab

clings to its cut?

Self-exilic, imaging
only the shadow, never the thing,
only the occultation
of these figures
of a self:
that crossing where the traffic light's
never green. Swamped
snag, the land
receding from it, at high tide; tide
always high. Glissandos, falling
scales, scales
falling from the eyes. Map-scales, and legends. Mapped

immensities—

*—My likeness,*
*There is something fierce and terrible in you,*
*eligible to burst forth*

And no one can tell

what it is—

Hence we remain ignorant
of the true shape, the mirror's
helpless,

deformed mirroring.

     \*

It's not the inside
of my body, not the shadow
of my liver at all,
not mine the five suspected
hemangiomas
the waves of the ultrasound
surround:

And so I draw
a self-portrait of withdrawal,
self-portrait as another's
concealed damage, my wife's
liver, shadowed, its textures

ambiguous, guessed-at . . .

     \*

*I want to make it like*

*but I don't know how to make it like*:
Bacon, on trying to reproduce
in paint a sea-wave

says he can only make it like
obliquely (fragmented,
blurred, other
than what it seems): *Because appearances*
*are ambiguous, this way of recording form*
*is nearer to the fact by its ambiguity of recording*—

What artificial
likenesses—equations, damaged

figures:
(a cosmology with $H_0 = 65$ km s$^{-1}$ Mpc$^{-1}$)
Bacon's self-portraits in half-face, the loathed
features marred with globes of black, waves
of excrescence, seceding

from figuration.

    \*

*What Makes Mr. Bruce Beasley Tick*:
personality portrait, compiled
by myself, on Mind Prober™ software
("A Complete X-ray of the Mind"):

*a great many fears over day-to-day matters*
*keeps people at an emotional distance*
*may seem remote and silent*
*likely to act uninterested*
*avoids most situations others would enjoy*
*once in a long while you may notice he comes out of his shell*

*you are likely to see him turn away*

    \*

In the beginning, Without End
took pleasure in Its own
autarkic self-sufficiency, there being

no other Being in the cosmos.
A shaking from Its isolation, as It coiled
deeper into Itself, having learned to need

an otherness, extra-
theos,

and so seceded

from what It made, imago Dei, birth-
contractions,
contracting into Its own birth

(You are likely to see Him

turn away)

What Einstein wanted most to know: Did God ever have a choice?


&ast;


And now the eruptive, the self
made of all its X-ray traces,
host galaxies, redshifting
billions of light-years away:
Kierkegaard: The self is the conscious synthesis
of finitude and infinitude,
whose task is to become itself,
which can only be accomplished in relationship to God. Augustine:
But where was I
when I looked for You?
You were there before my eyes, but I had deserted
even my own self. I could not find myself,
much less find You. Eckhart: Outside of God,
there is nothing but nothing.

Dickinson: Me from Myself—to banish/Had I Art—
How this be
Except by Abdication—

Me—Of Me—


&ast;

*What Makes Mr. Bruce Beasley*
*Tick*
(Mind Prober™ personality portrait,
compiled by my friends):

*Wants intensely to be showered with attention*
*A natural performer, happiest when he has the spotlight*
*The ultimate experience for him is to be sought after by others*
*Although he tries to maintain his cool, his self-control gives way*

*Going it alone is not for him*


\*


Autoluminosity, not-God

coming into being at the beginning of time
(nothing, but nothing)
gamma-rays' pilgrimage from then to now,
detected on December 14, 1997, at 5:34 p.m. CST
(an afterglow of $10^{53}$ erg, relativistic
ejecta)

Ejected
self, what the ultrasound can't see
(shadow, dark Mass unimaged)

celestial                                        "shocked gas"
          dimmed and reddened by dust

So dimmed,
dismembered
the metaphors of myself
(*zimzum*, gamma burst, mapped
immensities):

Shadow
of the hanging
scuppernong
where as a child I'd hide all day

Born
a twin, and as the moss
is ripped from a concrete wall,
what green
particles still cling

Drawbridge,
jutting its halves over the river

Crucifix: awkward
overlay of two broken sticks


                *


What kind of "parent object"
could give birth to such a blast:

Daddy in handcuffs, fire-
poker traced with blood

Mama's letters, script
palsied from vodka

Double-grave
by the crumbling mudbanks, kudzu's
creep across the dates

—*Always
disrupting this literalness,*
Bacon says,
*because I find it quite easy and quite uninteresting*

Eruptive,
       inward-
turning, against the literal,
the litter (lawn party,
little drinks with their umbrellas,
How is your summer going, are you taking any trips)
the shackled-
together letters of each word

(as the green
clings, the scab's
performed likeness to its cut)

Fuschia drinks left over, with their umbrellas, in the rain

The shackled-together letters of the Word
a millisecond after the Big Bang

Self-portrait as something
other, the waves
of the ultrasound
pound against

ambiguity—

Emergence
from occultation (shadow,
injured
image, turning
away):

*From distances and flux measurements*
*one can then infer*

*luminosities—*

V

# Errata Mystagogia

(*Summer Mystagogia*, 1996 Colorado Prize for Poetry)

There, in the misprints and vacant
pages, garbled
syntax of the proofreaders' spoils,

even the word *disfiguring* disfigured,
in the trail of twelve misspellings,
where adjectives cling to the wrong
nouns (*woodwasps*
instead of *dogwoods*
made pink),

I track the unfixable

everywhere, its slippery
letters, lessons
no one wants to know how to learn.

Where Augustine poses his question
so emphatically
it takes *two* question marks
to get it right:
*All these lovely but mutable*
*things, who has made them*
*but Beauty immutable??*

This mutable
book, its muted
voice, goes out to its warehouses and bookshops
with three pages gone,
second half of "The Reliquary Book"
(beginning "its passages
unmovably bound")

left blank, bound—
by the printwheels' skip—
to oblivion.
So I write this
errata sheet
for the uncorrectable proof
of all things: initiation
into the half-

hearted and bungled, *jug*
become *jog*, *beaks*
transfigured to *breaks*,
the *aggrsseive month for the ova*,
ellipses
inserted in the middle of a word
as though the lacuna
of language
couldn't help but bleed through . . .

*If Wallace Stevens had won the Colorado Prize,*

a friend tells me, *we'd be reading*
*"Anecdote of the Jog . . ."*

October, no apology from the editor,
no answer at all, word
of a relative
with water surrounding her heart, rain
dribbling from a birdbath where hollyhocks
shed the last of their pink
(woodwasps? erratum: blooms)

over a gash in the ground where a shallow-
rooted forsythia collapsed in a squall—

On the news, the usual
botch: Scrub of clearcut hills, hacked
groves of juniper and fir, cheery

senator posed over the saplings:
READY FOR HARVEST IN 2035—

Then a man
with a hatchet
left permanently in his head, its blade
too close to the brain

to remove.

*The book*
*broken*

in a mutable world, errata
inserted in the place of every page.

*for David Milofsky*

## Mutating Villanelle

Because God wants us to have indefinite life, like Him,
Richard Seed intends to electroshock an egg
to implant his image and likeness into Gloria, his wife

    (to implant into Gloria, his menopausal wife, his shocked image
       and likeness)

after inducing quiescence in its nucleus (moon-pause)
so his DNA might nest there and live forever,
cloned, and cloned, indefinite life God wants us to have, like Him.

Enucleated oocyte, like the lamb-clone Dolly's.
Lamb of God, who takes away the sins of the world,
(implanted sin, aboriginal, in the image and likeness of God, Gloria

in excelsis Deo) . . . *Heaven forbid,*
*I wouldn't trust him to breed a tadpole,* his ex-wife said.
God wants us like Him, in His image, after His likeness, seed

    (having shed "indefinite"
              having shocked into fusion the two mutating refrains)

fallen on fertilized ground. Nucleus hollowed, egg
shocked into taking the alien
cell into its image and likeness, glorious implantation.

        (lamb-
        clone, 237
        grotesque miscarriages
        before it was born)

*Lamb of God, you take away* our imperfections,
through manipulation of the flawed genes.
Because God wants us to be like Him, indefinite
    (because God wants us,

wants us clones of Him)
how soon will the womb of Gloria be implanted (*What rough beast*)
    with the image and likeness of seed . . .

    (Enucleated
    iambs, perfectible
    refrains [to hold oneself
    back, forbear],
    imperfectible rhymes
    [glory / story, likeness/
    Loch Ness]:
    grotesque
    miscarriage
            indefinite
            likeness,
    glory, electroshock, tadpole, rough beast, seed)

how soon will the womb of Gloria be implanted (*Hail, O favored one,*
    *the Lord is with thee)* with the image and likeness (fore-born) of
    Seed . . .

# The Monstrum Fugue

fugue: <Latin *fugere*, to chase, *fugare*, to flee:
1.  a polyphonic composition, constructed on one or more themes introduced from time to time with various contrapuntal devices
2.  a flight from one's own identity . . . a dissociative reaction to emotional stress, during which all awareness of personal identity is lost

*There are several things that cause monsters.*
*The first is the glory of God.*
—AMBROISE PARÉ

### Host

Imperfect
split of the ovum, flesh
fused, half doubled, half severed
*So the trumpettour soundit at such tyme*
*as the people sould cum and sie the Monster:*

Lazarus Colloredo,
the Italian Gentleman Pregnant
with His Brother

*that grows out of his navell*
*He carryes him at his syde*

Shrivelled
John Baptista, *which was borne with him,*
*and liveth still*, with rudimentary
genitalia, shared
viscera, liver, milt, &c., three fingers
on each hand, head
drooping backwards, torso half-
emerging, one leg
still buried in Lazarus's side

*It had a kynd of lyf, and feilling*

Sagged
lids. Feather-
stir to show he breathes.

Unsplit
into the imperfect, division

being wanted—

cognate: Lat. *com* (together) + *gnatus*, born
imperfect split

And the other

joined rupture:
multiple personality's
polyfragmentation, the psyche's
self-twinning, and twinning, in trauma, its
scattering the horror among the sharded
amnesiac selves,
each the keeper of one memory *(a kynd
of lyf, and feilling,
it liveth still)*

A deadbolted
room has been found
in Violet's mind, stinking
always of Lysol: the alters
huddle outside the door.
She's still
twelve in there,

gone mute from screaming unanswered for twenty years.

The multiples
watch from inside,
even when no one knows
they're there,

even when they can't speak . . .

Cum and sie the Monster,
multiplied,
both joined and separated:
Monster: <Lat. *monstrare,* to show, *monore,* to warn: a grotesquely
    abnormal fetus or infant
Monstrance: <Lat. *monstrum,* portent, monster: a receptacle that holds
    the Host

            (grotesquely
    abnormal, twinning, and twinning:)
Host: the consecrated bread of the Eucharist
Host: an organism that harbors a parasite
Host: a great multitude, as *a host of angels*
Host: in Multiple Personality Disorder, the alter personality most
    frequently in control of the body

Letter
from an alter to its host:
"I am the Stranger Within.
I possess and rule absolutely
all your thoughts and actions.
Your body is merely my mask for survival
amidst this gruesome world of humans . . ."

*And Lazarus concealed the body of his little brother*
*by covering it with his cloak*
*so that a stranger would have no suspicion*

*of the monster underneath*

## 1st Alter: Ergo Sumus

When the "ego glue"
loosens,
when the cogito
ruptures
("When we
were a little girl . . .")

the soul selects its teams,

the spirit helpers, the demons, head-
bangers, the babies in foetal position,
teenage boys, girl-
children, "discarnate ego-entities" who soar
above the hospital, draw
the doctor
a bird's-eye view,

and each team elects one spokesman
to emerge before the therapist
and "abreact"
the sundered
past (thirty spokespersonalities
to manage the 300 inside)—

       —hauling up
the sunken time,
they let the doctor talk them
out of existence: shorn
amnesias, ego surrenders.

*Who am we,*

asked a Host,
*and how do I talk
about myselves? English
has no cupped hands*

*to carry my meaning—*

Disaggregation, alter-creation
even in the midst of hunting
the alters down,
merging them, soul and body, with the host
(John Baptista's leg
still buried in his Lazarus's side)

Division
being *wanted*—

Cum and sie the Monster,
no cupped hands:
fugue chase
fugue flee

*And Nature yet remembers/What was so fugitive*


    \*


*I pictured something dark and slimy*
*where my soul should be*


    \*


*Application for marriage is denied*
*on grounds that the bride is a Siamese twin*


    \*


*And in a deformed body draw a resemblance to the Soules*
*deformity*

## 2nd Alter: To Wonder

The "Two-Headed Nightingale,"
Millie-Christine, born
slave twins, sold
for $30,000 ("for the two
strange lumps of humanity")
tapdanced to their own duets,
one alto, one basso profundo:
"A marvel to myself am I,
As well as all who passes by.
I love all things that God has done,
Whether I'm created two, or one."

*One*
*in conglutination of externall parts*
from the coccyx
to the sacrum

In sideshows, in dime museums,
before Queen Victoria, the double-
monster

danced

(*Themes*
*stated successively by a number of voices*)

Fugue: amnesiac
flight, and forgetting
repetitions
that chase, and flee

Waiting for the doctor
to cut him free,
Eng felt his blood congealing
as it poured into his brother's
dead body

cleave: to split or separate
cleave: to adhere or cling
cling: to resist separation

                    Divorce
proceedings:
"Daisy is a lovely girl,
but I guess I'm not the kind of fellow
that should be married to a Siamese twin.
I guess I'm kind of a hermit
when it comes to that"

And in a deformed language
draw a resemblance to the soules
deformity

A marvel to myself am I
marvel: <Lat. *mirari,* to wonder at
mirror: <Lat. *mirari,* to wonder at
mirage: <Lat. *mirari,* to wonder at

Skull and scalp
fused, necks
twisted downward so the twins
could never see each other's face

*Whether two, or one*
The mirror's
mirage

wonder: to have a feeling of awe or admiration
wonder: to be filled with doubt

Doubt's
there, in the mirror of wonder,
what wonder

never wanted to see
Cum, and sie the Monster

### 3rd Alter: Self-Conception

What was,
so fugitive,
what the hypnotized
amnesiac multiples have come to remember:

Mobile crematoria, through Iowa,
Satanic ritual's
cartilage and ash

*My father
hacking off my head
with an axe, when I was eight*

Cult
suicide commands, coded
into Hallmark cards and pansies

(Concealed
monsters, the memory's
imperfect

split)

     When the monstrance
is opened, the Host
is divided, becoming
incarnate
all over again

And there are recondite
rooms within
the mind

with mirrored doors

The hypnotist must tread the glass floor, record

the self-
conceiving image
(4,500 "personality fragments"
in one host, each
half the host, half
someone just born, who has no name)

(Incarnate all over again, the twins
could never see each other's face)

Each refusing
to "yield their separateness"
(yield: to put forth, furnish, exhibit;
yield: to hand over, relinquish, give up)

A resemblance
to deformity

Monster: to show, to warn
St. John the Baptist, forerunner,
always preparing the way

4 April 1637: *A license to Lazarus, to shew his brother Baptista*
Baptista's lips moved without sound
whenever Lazarus spoke
*What excrement he had was emitted from his own mouth*

A monster of duplex
symmetrical development
(Millie's heart mirrored Christine's:
one on the right of her chest,
one on the left)

Rectus    Inversus
In Bach's mirror fugues, a motive
stated in the soprano
recurs in the bass,
dominants replace tonics, tonics
return as dominants,
descending melodies reverse-
echo ascending ones

(a monstrance
of doubled
asymmetric development: trans-
substantiant wafer, echoed
in divine descending flesh)

*The Father is with the Son, and the Son with the Father*
*always and inseparably,*

Augustine says. Trying to unsnare the mystery
of the Trinity in words

(he said, in words)
was like trying to pour the whole ocean
into a hollow he'd scraped in the sand.

~~~

A man must leave his father and mother

and *cleave*

unto his wife:

—the Bride
is a Siamese twin—

Lazarus, come forth

———————————————

Man and wife must            twin
father-and-mother is          Siamese
his          Bride      forthcome

un-
    two

twin
twine

                  cleave
                  leave

~~~

What can't be
contained
in language (*contain*: to hold
together), the way the Father
contains the Son,
and the Spirit
encompasses both,

*always mutually in one another, neither is ever alone—*

(Motive
restated in the bass:)

*Remember God is a multiple, too,*

said a host,
*Father, Son, and Holy Spirit*

                              (The multiples
stare,

descending ...)

modulates from dominant to subdominant,
from mediant to sub-
mediant

(a showing, a warning
of halved
symmetrical disintegration)

*twin–twin transfusion syndrome*
*hypervolemia in one*
*omphalapagous twin*
*hypovolemia in the other*
*unbalanced shunting within the mutual circulation*

*Urgent separation of the conjoined*
*twins must be undertaken*

*5th Alter: Metaphor: to transfer, to "bear change"*

In the Ritual of Integration
("'Me' is 'We' reversed")
the twins must be
unblended, reabsorbed
into the body of the host
(the common gastrointestinal tract
divided beyond the terminal ileum,

dissociative shunting-aside
of painful amnesiac affects
must be ablated through undoing
discontinuities of identity and memory)

*They twain*
*shall be one flesh*
no more, cranium
severed, the double
liver
surgically torn asunder,

and the personalities
one by one
weaken, and die
(their blood congealed
in the twin's
dead body)
as the host
reassembles a cohesive memory—

But no
co-
hesion here: even
these metaphors
won't yield

separation:
multiple
personalities, conjoined
twins

cognates

the metaphors
cleaving

(So the double monster
could dance)

How
keep them apart:
Who is joined with an alter named Garbage?
Who fused
by a "sword-shaped appendix"
to a brother already stiffening with rigor mortis?

*Introduce me     to myself*

*6th Alter: Suicide*

      (If the double-metaphor
          won't "yield":

In autoimmune disorders, the cells
confuse themselves
for invading

pathogens, antigen
and antibody
deranged, so the

"self-tissues"
cannibalize themselves:
Not-I and I

indistinguishable (Who
am we), hyper-
aggressive, so

the Self, double-

monster, consumes its prey—

*7th Alter: X*

"Rosa liked sour things,
Josepha liked sweets.
Rosa had sex desire,
Josepha had none."

Leaning
always into each other,
their bodies formed a permanent X

       (an unknown or unnamed factor or thing)
       (to multiply)
       (to eliminate or cross out)

Autopsy
report (*auto* + *opsis*: self-
sight):

*A tongue-shaped*
*piece of tissue*
*in the lumen of the left vagina*

*bifurcating, and terminating, the common vaginal canal*

"Waltzing was one of their accomplishments.
Unquestionably their intestines were united."

Rosa's
baby suckled all four breasts

lumen: Lat., opening

X

bifurcate =
terminate

*Lyric*

Ineliminable

residuum
John Baptista, huddled

in the cloak
Listless, shut-

lidded
Lips stirring as I speak

The voice of One
in the wilderness

From my navel
he has dragged

Half-
emergent (labored

trace of the thorax)
No license

to shew
When the monstrance

is broken
into, when the Host

is split in two          This
is my body               Do

this,                    in memory
of me                    Lazarus, come

| | |
|---|---|
| forth | what |
| monster | have you brought |
| | |
| hidden there | what |
| trumpet | will they sound |
| | |
| Hallelujah | when the days |
| are spent | when the Lord |
| | |
| has split | the cursed from the |
| blest | at last |

in the time of the blending of antonyms:

Nicolas of Cusa: *The place wherein*
*Thou art found unveiled*

*is girt round with the coincidence*
*of contradictories,*

*there Thou mayest be seen*
*and nowhere this side thereof—*

This side, my
side, Baptista's leg

still buried there
Introduce me

to myself
(*intro* + *ducere*: to lead

within) in-
elimin-

| | |
|---|---|
| able trace | in- |
| viable terata— | |

I, Lazarus, gravid
with the swaddled

monster (*always*
*mutually in*

*one another*), division
being wanted, im-

perfect split, for the
shewing of the glory of God . . .

# Notes to the Poems

### Negatives of O'Connor and Serrano

In Flannery O'Conner's novel *Wise Blood*, Hazel Motes resists his calling to be a prophet by founding the Church of Truth Without Christ. Eventually he attempts to atone for his sin by blinding himself and mortifying his flesh with glass in his shoes and barbed wire around his waist. In her story "Good Country People," Joy Freeman changes her name to Hulga after losing her leg in an accident. She attempts to seduce a Bible salesman, who steals her wooden leg and abandons her in the loft of a barn.

Negative 1. The opening quotations are from Rep. Richard Armey of Texas (Andres Serrano would jack off on Jesus . . .) and from Sen. Jesse Helms of North Carolina ("What this Serrano fellow did . . .").

Negative 2. The parenthetical quotations are from Pseudo-Dionysius.

Negative 5. The Misfit, in O'Connor's "A Good Man Is Hard to Find," is an escaped killer who "can't make what all I done wrong fit all I gone through in punishment."

Negative 6. The hermaphrodite in a circus freak show appears in O'Connor's "A Temple of the Holy Ghost." Serrano has pickled brains in vials in his apartment in Brooklyn. Parker, in O'Connor's "Parker's Back," covers every surface of his skin with tattoos, finally having a massive Christ tattooed on his back.

Negative 8. The three unidentified quotations are from Pseudo-Dionysius.

### Sermons on Unbelief

II. "My heart and I have decided to end it all" is from Billie Holliday's song "Gloomy Sunday"; "O triumphant holy day" is from the traditional Easter hymn "Jesus Christ Is Risen Today."

III. "Che bel marmo hai rovinato": What beautiful marble you have ruined—Michelangelo's taunt to a rival sculptor, upon seeing his statue of Neptune: "Ammanato, Ammanato / Che bel marmo hai rovinato!"

### Spiritual Alphabet in Midsummer

A. In Exodus, God "hardens the heart" of Pharoah in order to manifest His wonders through a series of plagues against the Egyptians.

B. The quotations from Julian of Norwich are from her *Showings*.

F. Tetris, the popular video game, is played by arranging a series of rapidly falling geometric shapes into orderly rows.

H. The parable of the tares and the wheat is found in Matthew 13.

I. The quotations that begin and end the section are St. Paul from I Corinthians 15, as is "Lo, I tell you a mystery" at the beginning of the next section.

J. Excerpts from an interview with Pema Jones, the teenaged lama, appear in *Harper's Magazine*, August 1996.

M. The quotations from Cotton Mather and from Franz Kafka are from their diaries. A&E is the television Arts and Entertainment channel.

N. "Filled with the Devotions and Enjoyments of a raised soul" is from Cotton Mather's diary.

O. The opening quotation is from Mark 8:12.

P. Docetic heresy is the belief that Christ only appeared to have a physical body but in fact was purely spiritual.

Q. The Emily Dickinson quotation is from one of her letters.

R. The quotation is from a description of the devotion to the Sacred Heart of Jesus, from *The Catholic Encyclopedia*.

W. Michael Wigglesworth was a seventeenth-century Massachusetts Puritan. The quotations from him here are from his diaries.

Y. "Eli, Eli, lama sabachthani" (My God, my God, why have you forsaken me") are the words of Christ on the cross in Matthew 27:46.

The final quotation is from Verdi's *La Traviata*: "Let's drink . . . the fleeing hour yields to pleasure's intoxication."

Z. Ordinary Time constitutes the parts of the Catholic liturgical year in between the sacramental seasons of Advent, Christmas, and Easter.


### The Unburied

"Aspergillum" is the brush used for sprinkling holy water at Mass.


### Hermetic Self-Portrait

"Your hurt is incurable, sayeth the Lord . . .": Jeremiah 30.


### Damaged Self-Portrait

"My likeness/There is something fierce and terrible in you . . ." is a paraphrase from Whitman's "Earth, My Likeness."

ABOUT THE AUTHOR

Bruce Beasley is professor of English at Western Washington University. He has won fellowships from the National Endowment for the Arts and the Artist Trust and is the author of three books of poetry, including *Spirituals* (Wesleyan University Press). His second book, *The Creation*, received the 1993 Ohio State University Press / Journal Award, and his most recent collection, *Summer Mystagogia*, was selected by Charles Wright for the 1996 Colorado Prize. His poems have also appeared in *Kenyon Review, Ploughshares, Fence, Gettysburg Review*, and other journals, and in *The Pushcart Prize: Best of the Small Presses*.

LIBRARY OF CONGRESS CATALOGING-IN-PUBLICATION DATA

Beasley, Bruce, 1958–

  Signs and abominations / Bruce Beasley.

      p. cm. — (Wesleyan poetry)

  ISBN 0–8195–6455–9 (alk. paper) — ISBN 0–8195–6456–7 (pbk. : alk. paper)

  1. Religious poetry, American. 2. Art religion—Poetry. I. Title. II. Series.

  PS3552.E1748 S54 2000

  811'.54—dc21                                            00–009415